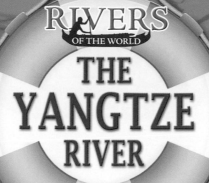

RIVERS
OF THE WORLD

THE
YANGTZE
RIVER

Earle Rice Jr.

Mitchell Lane
PUBLISHERS

P.O. Box 196
Hockessin, Delaware 19707

RIVERS
OF THE WORLD

The Amazon River

The Nile River

The Ganges River

The Mississippi River

The Rhine River

The Tigris (Euphrates) River

The Yangtze River

The Volga River

Copyright © 2013 by Mitchell Lane Publishers

All rights reserved. No part of this book may be reproduced without written permission from the publisher. Printed and bound in the United States of America.

PUBLISHER'S NOTE: The facts on which the story in this book is based have been thoroughly researched. Documentation of such research can be found on page 44. While every possible effort has been made to ensure accuracy, the publisher will not assume liability for damages caused by inaccuracies in the data, and makes no warranty on the accuracy of the information contained herein.

Printing   1   2   3   4   5   6   7   8   9

Library of Congress
Cataloging-in-Publication Data
Rice, Earle.
 The Yangtze river / by Earle Rice Jr.
    p. cm.—(Rivers of the world)
 Includes bibliographical references and index.
 ISBN 978-1-61228-299-2 (library bound)
 1. Yangtze River (China)—Juvenile literature. I. Title.
 DS793.Y3R54 2012 2013
 915.12—dc23
                                    2012009471
eBook ISBN: 9781612283722

                                    PLB

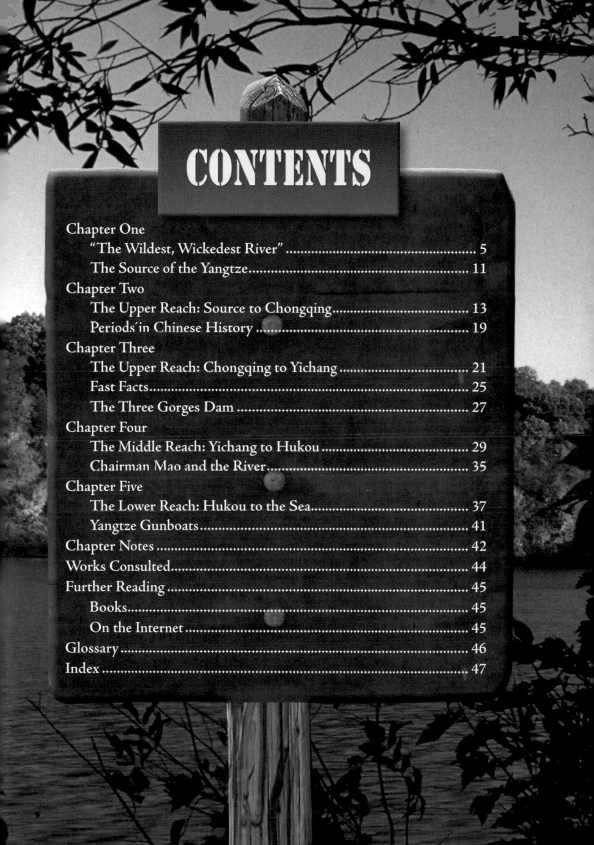

CONTENTS

The mighty Yangtze river at the
Qutang Gorge

CHAPTER 1

"The Wildest, Wickedest River"

Up a cobbled street in the Chinese river port of Zhenjiang (formerly known as Chinkiang), the Number One Radio Factory stands atop a hill overlooking the Yangtze River. Beside the plant, a small two-story house once rose almost unnoticed behind a barbed-wire fence. Long ago, a young American girl often sat at her window there above the Bund (river road) and stared out at the river for hours on end. She was something of a daydreamer. The many moods of China's great river seemed to match her own at any given time. Her solitary communes with the river offered a measure of calm amid the bustle and clamor of a busy seaport in a land far from her own.

As she grew up in Chinkiang, the river made a deep impression on her. She came to love it, fear it, respect it, and marvel at it. Compared to the Yangtze, even her native country's "Father of Waters"—the Mississippi River—seemed mild and small to her. She

The Sydenstriker family in 1901: Pearl, Absalom, Grace, and Caroline. Wang, the children's governess, stands behind.

would later confide, "there is no other river to equal [the Yangtze] for beauty and cruelty."[1]

This girl was the daughter of Absalom and Caroline Sydenstriker, who were Presbyterian missionaries from West Virginia. Her fifteen-year upbringing in China comprised an odd mix of East and West. She spoke both English and Chinese and enjoyed the care and company of a Chinese amah (female servant). Her playmates were Chinese, but her clothes and schooling were American. And she preferred scones with jam for tea over Chinese delicacies. "In those years," she recalled later, "I slipped instantaneously out of one life into another, depending upon the geography of the moment."[2] But throughout her youthful days, the river's flow supplied a constant in her life.

Her childhood hours in a far-off land soon slipped away. As a young lady, she returned to the United States to complete her education. She graduated Phi Beta Kappa (with high honors) in 1914 from Randolph-Macon Women's College in Lynchburg, Virginia. Modeling herself after her parents, she returned to China as a Presbyterian missionary. Three

Pearl Buck would later create the Pearl S. Buck Foundation, which sponsors funding for thousands of children in several Asian countries.

years later, she married John Buck, another missionary. They spent most of the next 17 years in China.

In 1927, her devotion to China and its people put her and her husband in mortal danger during the "Nanking Incident." The strange event involved a confused battle among Chinese Communist forces, Chiang Kai-shek's Nationalist troops, and warlords—all fighting for control of the city.

The Bucks perhaps owed their lives to a poor Chinese family who hid them while marauders looted their quarters. After a terrifying day in hiding, the Bucks were rescued by an American gunboat on the Yangtze River and ferried to Shanghai. Once again, China's great river had played an important role in the life of an American expatriate who grew up on its banks.

First edition of *The Good Earth.* It was the best-selling book of both 1931 and 1932.

By this time, this former child of China—Pearl S. Buck—had harnessed her daydreams and begun to write about what she knew best—China. She wrote about the Yangtze of her youth, which she called "the wildest, wickedest river upon the globe, and the most beautiful."[3] And she wrote about Wang Lung and his slave wife. Her tale of their rise and fall through famine and war and locusts won the Pulitzer Prize in 1932. She called her novel *The Good Earth*. Two more books dealing with Wang Lung's family soon followed. In 1938, she won the Nobel Prize for Literature.

Ms. Buck's many novels and beautiful prose earned her wide acclaim for opening up everyday life in China to Western readers. She wrote of Chinese peasants with love, sympathy, and a sure understanding of their lot in life. Pearl S. Buck is but one of countless writers who have featured the Yangtze in their writings. Yet millions of the river's tales go untold.

In China, those who live by the Yangtze River liken it to a dragon—that mythical monstrous winged and scaly serpent with a crested head and enormous claws. If the River Dragon could speak, he would tell of many tales. His anthology of stories would extend back to the Stone Age and talk about two million years of Chinese life. He would tell of 23 centuries of documented rule. And yet further back he would fantasize about another 10 centuries of earlier dynasties that now exist in legend only.

The Dragon's tales would center on the Yangtze River—China's *Chang Jiang* or "Long River"—for it is his home. It is also the dividing line between North and South China. The regions through which it and its tributaries flow provide home to some 350 million Chinese. Their lives and fortunes depend largely on the whims, fancies, and darker moods of an irascible river—a river personified by the capricious spirit of its own River Dragon.

In describing the relationship between the river and its mythical persona, author and adventurer Richard Bangs writes: "Its coils encircle the Middle Kingdom [China] in a deadly embrace, its serpentine course

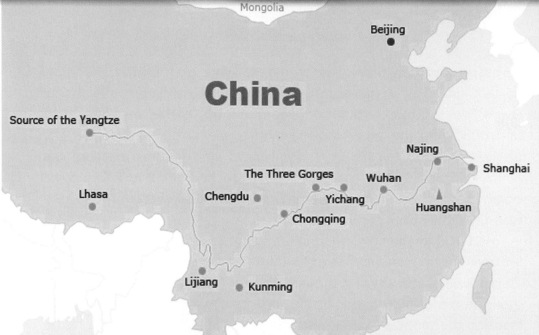

A map of the Yangtze river. The river starts from the western mountaintops, heads through the center of China, and ends just shy of Shanghai.

winds from high snowy lair to muddy wallow. The comparison with the dragon is not facile, but apt: the dragon in China is a monster, yes, but a life-giving, order-preserving monster."[4] But what it gives and preserves it also takes away and destroys when its mood turns dark.

In its temperate coastal climate, the Yangtze River Basin quite literally forms the rice bowl of China, producing 70 percent of the country's staple food item. It also yields cotton, wheat, barley, corn, beans, and other life-sustaining crops. Conversely, when the river's banks overflow with waters from melting snows and monsoonal rains, its ravaging floods can claim the lives of thousands of Chinese.

The River Dragon is both beneficent and beastly. He gives life and brings death. And he personifies "the wildest, wickedest river upon the globe, and the most beautiful."

The Source of the Yangtze

The glacier

In a remote and mostly closed country, the true source of the Yangtze went undiscovered until late in the 20th century. For many years, the Chinese believed the river's high and distant source lay in heaven. In 1976, an expedition of scientists from the China Geographic Institute in Beijing traced its origin to a trickle of ice water from the Jianggudiru Glacier on Mount Geladandong.

Mount Geladandong rises to a height of 21,723 feet (6,621 meters) in the Tanggula Mountains on the Qinghai-Tibet Plateau. The glacier's icy trickle drips and seeps to form a small lake called Qemo Ho. Waters from the lake stream into the Tuotuo He, or Murmuring River, and the Yangtze begins its run of almost 4,000 miles to the sea.

In 1985, the National Geographic Society sponsored a subsequent expedition. How Man Wong, a photographer/writer from Hong Kong, led the two-year exploratory mission. He followed the Dam Qu, a tributary of the Tuotuo He. Wong found that it started at a small, clear pool at the foot of a hill that the Tibetans call Jari. He claimed that this pool was the true source of the Yangtze.

Wong's discovery adds a mile to the overall length of the river. Though his claim has merit, not everyone accepts it. As writer Philip Wilkinson suggests, "for most people, the sheer magnificence of the glacial scenery around Mount Geladandong sways the debate so Jianggudiru is generally accepted as the primary source—the most remote and the most dramatic, if not quite the furthest from the East China Sea."[5]

The mountainous upper Yangtze

CHAPTER 2

The Upper Reach: Source to Chongqing

The Yangtze is China's longest, largest, and most famous river. It also ranks as the third longest river in the world. Only the Nile in Africa and the Amazon in South America are longer. The river's precise length varies from source to source. The most recent statistics place its length as just under 4,000 miles (6,437 km). Its height at its source is about 20,000 feet (6,096 meters).

The river flows through nine provinces: Tibet, Qinghai, Yunnan, Sichuan, Hubei, Hunan, Jiangxi, Anhui, and Jiangsu. Because of the Yangtze's great length, the locals give it several names along its winding course. It is usually divided into three parts known as the upper, middle, and lower reaches.

From its source to the city of Yichang, the Upper Reach is the longest, the wildest, and the most beautiful of the river's three sections. Its pristine landscape includes towering mountain ranges, deep ravines, untamed rapids, and raging torrents. Over this stretch of some 2,700 miles (4,345 kilometers),

Tanggula glacier

the river descends very sharply, losing about 95 percent of its original elevation.

Starting in the Tanggula Mountains, a trickle of melting glacier water widens and becomes the Tuotuo He (Murmuring River). It runs eastward through snowy hills. In the summer, the river swells with the glacial runoff, and the area turns into lush green marshlands called the "murmuring marshes." An ever-present sound of flowing water gives the name to both the marshes and the river.

Continuing eastward, it merges with the Dam Qu to form the broad upper reaches of the Tongtian He (River to Heaven). Wildlife of various kinds find drinking water and grazing lands here on the Qinghai-Tibet Plateau—antelope, wild yaks, ducks, and asses, geese, lynx, white-lipped deer, and more. Tibetan herdsmen tend their herds of yaks and deer, and farmers cultivate the flatlands for highland barley called *qingke*—the staple of Tibetan diets. Here the river freezes over from October to May.

Turning southeasterly near Yushu, the river takes the local name of Jinsha Jiang, or River of Golden Sand. Here it contains just enough gold flakes to account for its name and yellowish waters. While boating upstream on the Jinsha, author Simon Winchester noted that "it was rarely more than a hundred feet across, and the banks were steep and all the rapids merged into one, so the whole river frothed and boiled as we sped by."[1]

Flowing southward, the Jinsha plunges off the Qinghai-Tibet Plateau. Locals know the plateau as the "Roof of the World." For the next 1,400 miles (2,253 kilometers), the river forms the border between Sichuan and Tibet. It dips down into Yunnan Province, then loops back into Sichuan. On its southward sweep, it runs parallel to three other

First Bend in the Yangtze at Yunan

great rivers—the Mekong, the Salween, and the eastern branch of the Irrawaddy. At Shigu (meaning Stone Drum) in Yunnan Province, the river switches back sharply in a U-turn. This turn is called the First Bend. Here the Jinsha actually flows parallel to itself, separated by only 15 miles (24 kilometers).

In this area of breathtaking beauty, sloping forests of pine and spruce give way to alpine meadows of moss, blue gentians, and white edelweiss. Hemlock and flowering rhododendron bushes add to its natural splendor. Today, Tibeto-Burmese peoples live here as they have for centuries. They cultivate barley, wheat, vegetables, and indigo, and tend sheep or pigs.

The almost unbelievable colors of the Yunan province roll on the hills for miles.

During the 1920s, Austro-American botanist and explorer Joseph F. Rock headed an expedition to Yunnan Province for the National Geographic Society. He became the first Westerner to explore and photograph the region extensively. His photographs still delight and amaze viewers.

East of Shigu, the majestic Jade Dragon Snow Mountain can be seen on a rare cloudless day. It rises over the plain of Lijiang to a height of 18,400 feet (5,608 meters). This area is home to the Naxi people, one of China's indigenous groups.

On the north side of the mountain, the Jinsha passes through the deepest and most fearsome gorge of the entire river—the Tiger Leaping Gorge. As described by Simon Winchester, "the river squeezes itself through a twelve-mile cleft that in places is no more than fifty feet across: narrow enough, some say, for a tiger fleeing from a hunter to have once jumped clear across."[2] Cliffs on both sides of the gorge rise to the dizzying height of 12,800 feet (3,900 meters) in places.

Farther on, the Jinsha again plunges south, turns east, and finally swings northeast toward Yibin and Chongqing. Rushing through the province of Sichuan, the river picks up the flow of three major tributaries—the Min and the Jialing from the north, and the Wu from the south. These linkages give name to the province of Sichuan, which means "Four Rivers." As the Jinsha carves its way through mud and mountainsides, its surging waters pick up silt that fertilizes vegetation in valleys further downstream.

After the Min joins the Jinsha at Yibin, locals know the river as the Chang Jiang (Long River). The 1,640-foot high (500 meters) Sichuan or Red Basin enjoys mild winters and a long rainy season. Its rich agricultural lands have long produced cotton, hemp, and silk, as well as an abundance of grain. Five and a half million Yi—another indigenous group of peoples—live among the mountains of northeastern Yunnan and southeastern Sichuan.

Downstream, where the Jialing meets the Chang, Chongqing clings to steep cliffs. One of China's most important cities, it was allegedly

Chongqing

founded by the Ba people during the eleventh century BCE. Its name means "Double Celebration," after the crowning of a king of the Southern Song dynasty in 1189 CE. Chongqing has always played an important role in Chinese history. In modern times, the mountain city served as China's capital during the Second Sino-Japanese War (1937–45).

"It was a difficult time, when squadrons of Japanese bombers flew in and obliterated whole areas of Chinese cities," noted Philip Wilkinson. "But Chongqing was better defended than most—not just by its mountainous setting, but by its frequent fogs, which caused numerous Japanese raids to go off course and miss their targets."[3] Man-made caves that once provided shelter from enemy bombers still dot the Chongqing hills. They now serve as garages or restaurants and hair salons in their naturally cool settings.

In 1996, Chinese authorities granted Chongqing national status as a municipal region similar to Beijing, Shanghai, and Tianjin. With the opening of the colossal Three Gorges Dam below the city in 2006, really large ships can now navigate as far upriver as Chongqing. This old inland city promises to soon become one of the world's major ports.

Periods in Chinese History

Flag of China

Chinese civilization existed in the Huang (Yellow) River Valley as early as ca. 3000 BCE and probably spread from there. China's traditional history begins with the Hsia dynasty, ca. 2000 BCE. The Shang dynasty followed four hundred years later. It invented a writing system and began validating China's history for the first time in the written word.

Over its long history, China passed through alternating periods of upheaval and advancement. Notable among the former were the Warring States, the Three Kingdoms, and the Five Dynasties periods. China's so-called Golden Age of art and literature began under the Tang dynasty. Cultural achievements flourished during the Song period. Each of the dynasties and historical periods listed below contributed to the development of what is known today as the Peoples Republic of China.

Shang c.1600–1027 BCE
Western Zhou 1027–771 BCE
Eastern Zhou 770–256 BCE
Spring and Autumn 770–476 BCE
Warring States 475–221 BCE
Qin 221–207 BCE
Western Han 206 BCE–8 CE
Xin 9–24
Eastern Han 25-220
Three Kingdoms 220–265
Western Jin   265–316
Period of Disnity 317–618
Tang 618–907
Five Dynasties 907–960
Song 960–1279
Yuan (Mongol) 1279–1368
Ming 1368–1644
Qing (Manchu) 1644–1911
Chinese Republic 1912–1949
People's Republic of China 1949–

Chinese boats on the
Yangtze at the Three
Gorges

CHAPTER 3

The Upper Reach: Chongqing to Yichang

Continuing its northeasterly course along the Upper Reach, the Chang Jiang (Yangtze) flows past the cities of Fuling, Fengdu, and Wanxian. Between the major port of Chongqing and the scenic panorama of the gorges, vessels in a wide variety of shapes and sizes—from oceangoing ships to ever-present Chinese junks and sampans—jam this busy waterway.

The river Wu joins the Chang at the old town of Fuling. Historically, boatmen here have kept a careful watch on water levels. Jagged rocks beneath the surface might wreck their boats at low water. To track the river's rise and fall, locals created a unique scale: they carved fourteen fish on nearby White Crane Ridge which are visible only at low water. Some carvings date back to the Tang dynasty (618–907). Local farmers put their faith in an old saying that promises: "Stone fish appear, good harvest here."[1] When the dam at Three Gorges further downstream began operations, rising water levels covered the original carvings and new ones were carved higher up.

The city of Fengdu is the best place where people can learn about the Chinese ghost culture that permeates the place.

Fengdu, the next notable city along the river, was once known as the "City of Ghosts." During the Han dynasty (206 BCE–220 CE), two officials named Yin and Wang became Taoist recluses here and eventually were known as Immortals (spiritual beings). Together, their names mean "King of the Underworld." Boatmen, fearing attacks by their spirits, refused to moor their boats along the riverbank and anchored in midstream. Fengdu's "ghostly" reputation grew larger over the years. Later, for the sum of one dollar, pilgrims could buy a "Passport to Heaven," stamped by a city official and an abbot.

About two hours downriver from Fengdu, two nine-storied pagodas ensure good fortune for the silk-spinning city of Wanxian. Known as the Gateway to East Sichuan, it sits high above the river and spreads out on both sides of it. "Wanxian is an inauspicious-looking place," observed Simon Winchester, "and few passersby give it more than a glance."[2] In 1926, however, the city scratched out a minor mark in history. When a local warlord took to hijacking foreign vessels, two British gunboats shelled the city. In the event known as the Wanxian Incident, seven British sailors died and, by some estimates, about three thousand Chinese.

Some 277 miles (446 kilometers) downriver from Chongqing, the old walled city of Fengjie guards the mouth of Qutang Gorge. Qutang is the first of the Chang's storied Three Gorges, or *Sanxia* in Chinese. The other two are Wu and Xiling. Writers and travelers often compare the Three Gorges with America's Grand Canyon.

Fengjie has long been noted for building boats, particularly junks. More recently, it has become a regional industrial center producing silk, cement, and fertilizer. In olden times, the city often provided a temporary home to poets. Few lacked for inspiration at the imposing entrance to Qutang Gorge. Tang dynasty poet Li Po (701–762) once captured the atmosphere at the approach to the first of the Three Gorges on a downriver voyage:

> *Downstream to Jiangling we do a thousand li a day!*
> *Monkeys cling to the cliffs, no end to their screeching.*
> *Ten thousand folded mountains our boat passes on its way.*[3]

Li Po may have exaggerated. A thousand *li*—about 311 miles or 500 kilometers—and 10,000 mountains represent a lot of miles traveled and mountains passed in one day. An aura of expectation at this threshold of scenic wonder may have triggered his sense of poetic license.

As the river enters the five-mile-long Qutang (or Wind Box) Gorge, it narrows to about 330 feet (100 meters). It is the shortest of the three gorges through which the river flows for the next 150 miles (241 kilometers), reaching a velocity of up to 15 miles (25 kilometers) an hour. Its sheer cliffs, often draped in mist, rise to about 4,000 feet (1,200 meters) on either side of the river. "Above the waters, tracker trails were cut into the cliffs where hundreds of men once heaved on bamboo

Hauling Chinese junks up the Yangtze

hawsers to haul junks up the rapids,"[4] notes author Richard Perry Hayman, who has traveled the river many times.

In 1971, several wooden coffins were found hanging from a cliff face along this stretch of the river. They contain the remains of members of the Ba tribe who lived in the region during the Warring States period (475–221 BCE). The coffins remind passers-by of the imminence of death and danger.

About 25 miles (40 kilometers) below Qutang, the new city of Wushan marks the start of the second gorge. Wu (Witches') Gorge, the most beautiful of the Three Gorges, twists and turns through the Wushan Mountains for 28 miles (45 kilometers).

A folk tale holds that Yao Ji, daughter of the Queen Mother of the West, protected the boatmen and people along the river in this area

FAST FACTS

- The Yangtze River is the longest river in Asia, with a length of 3,915 miles (6,300 kilometers), and the third longest river in the world after the Nile and the Amazon.

- The Yangtze River Basin extends for about 2,000 miles (3,219 kilometers) from east to west and for more than 600 miles (966 kilometers) from north to south.

- The Yangtze River Basin drains an estimated area of 700,000 square miles (1,126,510 square kilometers), one-fifth of China's total land area, and affects the lives of more than 400 million people.

- Eight principal tributaries flow into the Yangtze River from source to mouth: the Yalung, Min, Chialing, and Han rivers on the left bank; the Wu, Yuan, Hsiang, and Kan rivers on the right bank.

- The Yangtze carries approximately 35.3 trillion cubic feet (99.9 trillion cubic meters) of water to the sea annually, and discharges 530 million tons (538.5 metric tons) of yellow silt into the Yellow Sea.

- The Three Gorges (west to east) are located in the Upper Reach of the Yangtze: Qutang and Wu in Sichuan Province, Xiling Gorge in Hubei Province.

- The Three Gorges Dam raised the water level by approximately 360 feet (110 meters) to a total depth of 574 feet (175 meters) at the dam site at Sandouping in Xiling Gorge.

- The Three Gorges Dam created a 360-mile-long (579-kilometer) reservoir, which is approximately the same length as Lake Superior.

- The Three Gorges Dam forced the relocation of 1.2 million people or more.

Goddess Peak

from 12 dragons which were wreaking havoc and causing floods. Yao Ji and her 11 maidens tamed the dragons and now watch over the river in the eternal form of Goddess Peak, which resembles a kneeling maiden and stands about 3,000 feet high (940 meters), and 11 nearby sculpted peaks.

Xiling, the third and last gorge, is the longest of the three. It extends for 47 miles (76 kilometers), through the most violent stretch of the Chang (Yangtze). At the lower end of the gorge, a section of towering rocks and dramatic scenery, the effects of recent man-made changes become clear. "Only a short distance of jagged rocks and soaring peaks remain before Sandouping," writes Philip Wilkinson, "the site of the Three Gorges Dam itself."[5] Finally, just beyond the lesser Gezhouba Dam—completed in 1988—the Chang arrives at Yichang, 2,700 miles (4,345 kilometers) downriver from its source.

The Three Gorges Dam

Three Gorges Dam

Chinese leader Sun Yat–sen originally proposed the colossal Three Gorges Dam in 1919. His vision passed to his successor, Chiang Kai-shek, whose preliminary work was put aside when war broke out with Japan. Communist leader Mao Zedong supported the project after coming to power in 1949, but he decided to build the Gezhouba Dam first. Economic problems delayed further development of the larger dam for several decades.

After years of planning and debate, the National People's Congress approved the project with a mixed vote in 1992. Construction began on the Three Gorges Dam in 1994. It started up in 2006 and became fully operational in 2011.

The dam stands 607 feet (185 meters) high and holds back a body of water about 575 feet (175 meters) deep. Sometimes called the "Great Wall across the River," its span across the Yangtze measures 7,661 feet (2,335 meters). This massive barrier creates a reservoir that extends upstream 410 miles (660 kilometers) to Chongqing.

Proponents of the dam point to its annual electricity generation of more than 100 TWh (terawatt hours) of clean energy, improved shipping, and its lifesaving flood-control capability. Its detractors criticize the dam's expense of some $30 billion—including the cost of relocating some 1.2 million people—its negative effect on the environment and wildlife, and its potential for disaster in the event of a break. Whether the dam will prove to be a boon or a boondoggle to the Chinese people must await the test of time.

Yichang farmland

CHAPTER 4

The Middle Reach: Yichang to Hukou

Yichang marks the end of the Upper Reach and the beginning of the Middle Reach. Here the river emerges from the mountains and rocky gorges and flows through the lowland plains of east-central China. It slows, broadens, and runs downstream for about 600 miles (966 kilometers) to Hukou at the mouth of Poyang Lake. Three main tributaries—the Yuan, Xiang, and Han—and many smaller ones join the Yangtze in this region, which contains most of the Yangtze basin's crop production and population.

"I Chang [now Yichang], with all its squalor, its aloofness, and its proud self-sufficiency, is one of the most characteristically Chinese cities in the whole country," asserted G.R.G. Worcester at the beginning of the war years. As a river inspector of the Chinese Maritime Customs on the Yangtze for more than 30 years, he formed his impressions firsthand. "The variety of its scenery, the carefully guarded traditions, the interest of its boats and the courage of the

Traditional Chinese junk

junkmen, all make it a fascinating centre for anyone interested in the age-old culture of China."[1]

Yichang's history dates back for more than two thousand years. During the Three Kingdoms period (220–265), the armies of the Wu and Shu Kingdoms clashed in a famous battle. A Wu army of 50,000 troops set fire to the Shu encampment and routed the much larger Shu army of 700,000 men. Yichang's recent history includes sackings by Chinese bandits on two occasions and a five-year occupation by Japanese troops. The Japanese used the city as a staging area for bombing Chongqing.

Yichang owes much of its recent growth and prosperity to the construction of the Gezhouba Dam. Chairman Mao Zedong approved the project in 1970. Its construction served as a sort of practice run for the much larger Three Gorges Dam to follow. After eighteen years of construction and many redesigns, the Gezhouba Dam was finished in 1989. It stands 177 feet (54 meters) high, extends 8,550 feet (2,606 meters) across, and holds back 56 billion cubic feet (1.58 cubic mebers) of water. Its generators produce over 15 billion kilowatts of electricity a year.

On the down side, the construction of new dams has disrupted the breeding cycle of the endangered Chinese sturgeon. Other species at risk include the Chinese alligator, the finless porpoise, and the Chinese paddlefish. The *Baiji,* or Chinese river dolphin, has already been declared extinct.

About 30 miles (48 kilometers) downstream from Yichang, the river meanders across the Jianghan Plain and arrives at the twin cities of

Chinese sturgeon

Jingzhou and Shashi. Jingzhou, previously known as Jiangling, was a regional capital as early as 2000 BCE. It served as the capital of the Kingdom of Chu in the Spring and Autumn period (770–476 BCE) and as a chief city during the Three Kingdoms period. Regional dwellers still honor Guan Yu (c.160–219 BCE), a courageous local warrior, as the god of war.

Shashi, once a port for Jingzhou, now eclipses its sister city in size, population, and manufacturing enterprises. They include cotton mills, machinery, light consumer goods, printing, and dyeing and textiles. A strongly religious city, Shashi became a center of Buddhism during the Tang dynasty (618–907). Just west of the city, the seven-storied Wanshoubao Pagoda, built during the Ming dynasty (1368–1644), still watches over the waterfront though many others have disappeared.

For the next 200 miles (320 kilometers), the Yangtze twists and turns toward Dongting Lake. Along its winding path, it flows through silt-rich plains dotted with villages and paddy fields stocked with grazing water buffalo. Dongting, at 1,160 square miles (3,000 square

A water buffalo with a calf enjoying a bath in Southern Jiangxia District, City of Wuhan

kilometers), is the second largest of China's lakes. It abounds in fish and acts as a reservoir for summer flood waters.

Nearby, a sharp escarpment known as Red Cliffs commemorates a classic battle of the same name. The clash pitted the huge forces of Wei against the combined lesser armies of Shu and Wu. It took place in either 208 or 209, during the Eastern Han dynasty (25–220). The latter forces prevailed under the shrewd leadership of legendary hero Zhuge Liang. Weapons of the battle are still on display at the site, making Red Cliffs a huge tourist attraction.

Meandering on through a watery countryside often obscured by protective raised banks, the Yangtze arrives at Wuhan at the junction of the Han River. "From a distance, Wuhan looks like a big modern city, its skyscrapers and shops glistening with the high-tech sheen of twenty-first century China," writes Philip Wilkinson. "But it is actually three cities in one—Hankou, Wuchang, and Hanyang—and each of these places, which have grown and gradually merged together, has its own identity and history."[2]

The Yellow Crane Tower was rebuilt in 1981 and looks very different from the original one, but it still impresses thousands of tourists each year.

Hankou is a former Treaty Port renowned in the past for its exports of tea and opium, and now as a trade center. Hanyang shares the north bank of the Yangtze with Hankou, separated from it by the Han River. Wuchang, the oldest of the three cities, sits on the Yangtze's south bank. The old city is the site of the Yellow Crane Tower. Its name comes from a tale about a Taoist sage who was carried off to immortality by a crane. People in Wuchang now regard the crane as a symbol of long life. In 1956, the tri-city of Wuhan gained recent fame as the place where Chairman Mao Zedong swam across the Yangtze.

The Middle Reach of the Yangtze ends 140 miles (225 kilometers) south of Wuhan at the town of Hukou. Resuming its northeasterly course, the river begins its final 600 mile (966 kilometers) run to the sea.

Chairman Mao and the River

Mao Zedong

China's Long River profoundly influenced the life of Chinese leader Mao Zedong, both directly and symbolically. Mao served as chairman of both the Chinese Communist Party (1931–76) and the People's Republic of China (1949–59). Throughout his career, he felt drawn to the rushing current that had helped to preserve and sustain him.

Mao became a committed Marxist (communist) in 1921. By 1925, he had become convinced that the Chinese peasantry held the key to a successful Marxist revolution. As chairman of the Chinese Soviet Party, he began to mobilize the peasants in rural Jiangxi Province. In the early 1930s, Mao and his Red Army suffered repeated attacks by Chiang Kai-shek's Nationalist armies. Mao was forced to flee to the west with about 85,000 troops. So began what came to be called the Long March.

Mao and his ragtag army arrived at Jiaopingdu in April 1935 and boated across the Yangtze to safety in Shaanxi Province. Their numbers had dwindled to about 8,000 survivors. But Mao held his band together. He had led them across rugged mountains and the Long River itself. And he had proved he could earn the loyalty and devotion of the peasantry. Most important, he had shared their struggle and *inspired* them. Mao had turned a temporary defeat into an ultimate victory.

In 1956, Mao, then the supreme Chinese leader, swam the perilous waters of the Yangtze at Wuhan to restore a waning public confidence in his leadership. His risky and dramatic gesture helped to rekindle his image as a fit and fiery revolutionary leader.

The colorful everglade by Poyang Lake, the largest
fresh water lake in the country.

CHAPTER 5

The Lower Reach: Hukou to the Sea

The small, little-known town of Hukou sits at the entrance to Lake Poyang, the largest lake in China. Poyang's size increases during the flood season and shrinks in winter. It covers a surface area of about 1,930 square miles (5,000 sq kilometers). Its waters teem with fish, including mandarin, anchovy, and whitebait. On the western end of the lake, a 54,000-acre (22,000-hectare) nature reserve hosts some 4,000 cranes, 40,000 swan geese, and 250,000 ducks. More than 90 percent of the world's Siberian cranes make their home in the rich wetlands here.

The Yangtze further widens here in its final sweep to the sea. It skirts northern Jiangxi and traverses the provinces of Anhui and Jiangsu. A flat delta plain crisscrossed by canals and waterways typifies the river's Lower Reach. Its rich soil and profuse water resources give rise to the region's centuries-old name as the "Land of Fish and Water."

This wetland produces about 70 percent of China's rice crop and nearly half of its fish catch. Fish

Fishermen on Poyang Lake encounter many species of exotic fish.

in this section of the river include anchovies, carp, whitefish, and catfish. Fishing provides food and a source of income for river dwellers. They fish with trained cormorants (web-footed water birds) and various kinds of nets—bag-like fyke nets, drop nets, or long damming nets. But recent changes have put this lifestyle at risk.

"A combination of water pollution and over-fishing has led to a decline in fish stocks and seasonal bans on fishing,"[1] notes Philip Wilkinson. Further, the potentially adverse effects of the Three Gorges Dam on the ecosystem require constant monitoring.

Anqing, the first city along the lower reach, sits along the Dalong Hills on the river's north bank. An old city, it was capital of Anhui Province during the Qing dynasty (1644–1911) and the Republican period (1911–49). Rebels occupied the city for six years during the Taiping Rebellion (1850–64). In 1853, Qing emperor Xianfeng wondered "how could that important provincial capital be captured by bandits in one day?"[2] Bandits razed most of the city. It remained in ruins until after the turn of the century.

Below Anqing, the Yangtze winds for another 60 miles (100 kilometers) to the city of Wuhu. It is located on the river's south bank at the junction of the Qingi River. The city was once a great rice-marketing center, until bandit activity during the 1920s and 1930s stifled trade. It now produces light-industrial goods and serves as a transportation hub.

About another sixty miles along the river's path stands Nanjing, also on the south bank of the river. This city, whose name means "Southern Capital," is the present capital of Jiangsu Province. "Very few places in China have soared and plummeted with such fantastic and tragic recklessness," writes Simon Winchester. "The city was the glorious capital of some dynasties and then remaindered as a dusty and provincial backwater for others."[3] Today, as an industrial city of about 4.5 million people, it has regained some of its past glories.

In 1968, Chinese engineers entered the twentieth century when they completed the Nanjing Yangtze River Bridge. It is the first bridge to span the Lower Reach of the river. It is also the first double-decker, double-track highway and railway bridge to be designed and built entirely by the Chinese without outside assistance. Tidal waters begin at Nanjing, creating a drastic shift in water levels. So, according to Simon Winchester, the bridges buttresses and columns "have to withstand the river's current, the sea's tides, the estuary's bores, and a range in water height that is unknown on any river elsewhere on the planet."[4]

About an hour downriver from Nanjing, the Yangtze flows by the cobbled streets and alleys of Zhenjiang. A wide array of junks and sampans populate the river in this section where U.S. gunboats once patrolled and protected American interests. Zhenjiang, the onetime

15-year residence of Pearl S. Buck, is perhaps better known as the place where the Grand Canal joins the Yangtze.

Like China's Great Wall, the Grand Canal was built in different periods beginning as early as the fourth century BCE. At 1,085 miles (1,747 kilometers) in length, it is the world's longest manmade waterway. It links Beijing with the Yangtze, making Zhenjiang one of the most important transport hubs on the river.

Finally, China's Long River reaches the East China Sea, almost 4,000 miles from its source in the Qinghai-Tibet Plateau. As is the case with many great rivers, a great city rises near its mouth: Shanghai sits on the Huangpu River, about 13 miles from the mouth of the Yangtze. Like many great cities, it has known good times and not-so-good times. During the 1930s, Shanghai ranked among the world's ten largest cities. It flourished as a city of commerce and a multinational hub of finance and business. After the Communist Party takeover of the Chinese mainland in 1949, the once-vibrant city fell into decline. But it came back strong.

"Since 1975 the official number of people living in China's most populous city—dubbed 'New York on steroids'—has almost doubled,"[5] observed Brook Larmer, a former Shanghai bureau chief for *Newsweek* magazine.

More than six million migrants have raised the city's total population to 20 million. And its area has increased in size by almost 400 square miles (1,036 square kilometers). Today's Shanghai has recaptured its status as a global city. It influences China's commerce, finance, technology, fashion, and culture. And it is well on its way to becoming an international financial hub and shipping center in the near future.

"Modern Shanghai," notes travel writer Charis Chan, "owes its development, cityscape, and pre-eminence to that strange concoction of Western traders and regional Chinese entrepreneurs who flocked to Shanghai and together made it their home and their fortune."[6] More than anything else, perhaps, Shanghai owes its resurgence to its location near the mouth of China's Long River.

Yangtze Gunboats

Gunboat

For most of China's long existence, the Chinese exhibited little interest in foreign trade. Their attitude changed rapidly after two 19th century trading wars known as the Opium Wars. The first of these wars was fought between China and Great Britain (1839-42); the second, between China and a British-French alliance (1856–60). Western victories in both encounters yielded trade treaties with China. These agreements opened the door wide to Western commerce. The Yangtze River became the main trading avenue into inland China.

American interests in China grew fast. In the 1870s, the United States created an "Asiatic Fleet" to protect merchant ships against marauding river pirates and warlords. Before the turn of the century, foreign warships—mostly British and American—became commonplace on the lower reaches of the Yangtze River.

Early in the 20th century, the Standard Oil Company began operating tankers on the river. About 1914, specially built, shallow-draft gunboats advanced upriver as far as Chungking (Chongqing), more than 1,300 miles (2,092 kilometers) inland.

In 1926–27, Chinese government forces battled warlords during the Chiang Kai-shek's "Northern Expedition." Chaos reigned in China. To reinforce its Asiatic Fleet, the U.S. Navy added six new shallow-draft gunboats to its "Yangtze Patrol." American author Richard McKenna based his book *The Sand Pebbles* on one such gunboat caught up in the chaos of the Northern Expedition. And failing her rescue by a U.S. gunboat, Pearl S. Buck might not have lived to write her prize-winning novel *The Good Earth*.

Chapter 1 The Wildest, Wickedest River
1. Pearl S. Buck, *"The Wildest, Wickedest River,"* in *Yangtze River: The Wildest, Wickedest River on Earth.* Edited by Madeleine Lynn (New York: Oxford University Press, 1997), p. 42.
2. Ibid., p. 37.
3. Ibid., p. 41.
4. Richard Bangs and Christian Kallen, *Riding the Dragon's Back: The Race to Raft the Upper Yangtze* (New York: Atheneum, 1988), p. 6.
5. Philip Wilkinson, *Yangtze* (London: BBC Books, 2005), p. 22.

Chapter 2 The Upper Reach: Source to Chongqing
1. Simon Winchester, *The River at the Center of the World: A Journey Up the Yangtze and Back in Chinese Time* (New York: Henry Holt and Company, 1997), p. 288.
2. Ibid., p. 333.
3. Philip Wilkinson, *Yangtze* (London: BBC Books, 2005), p. 49.

Chapter 3 The Upper Reach: Chongqing to Yichang
1. Philip Wilkinson, *Yangtze* (London: BBC Books, 2005), p. 57.
2. Simon Winchester, *The River at the Center of the World: A Journey Up the Yangtze and Back in Chinese Time* (New York: Henry Holt and Company, 1997), p. 273.
3. Wilkinson, p. 60.
4. Richard Perry Hayman, *Three Gorges of the Yangzi: Grand Canyons of China* (New York: Odyssey Publications, 2000), pp. 11–12.
5. Wilkinson, p. 81.

Chapter 4 The Middle Reach: Yichang to Hukou
1. Deirdre Chetham, *Before the Deluge: The Vanishing World of the Yangtze's Three Gorges* (New York: Palgrave MacMillan, 2002), p. 110.
2. Philip Wilkinson, Yangtze (London: BBC Books, 2005), p. 108.

Chapter 5 The Lower Reach: Hukou to the Sea

1. Philip Wilkinson, *Yangtze* (London: BBC Books, 2005), p. 133.
2. Judy Bonavia, *The Yangzi River*. Revised by William Hurst (Lincolnwood, Illinois: Passport Books, 1997), p. 121.
3. Simon Winchester, *The River at the Center of the World: A Journey Up the Yangtze and Back in Chinese Time* (New York: Henry Holt and Company, 1997), p. 115.
4. Ibid., p. 119.
5. Brook Larmer, "Shanghai Dreams." *National Geographic,* Vol. 217 – No. 3 March 2010, p. 132.
6. Charis Chan, *An Illustrated Guide to China* (Hong Kong: The Guidebook Company, 1988), p. 112.

Boating on the Yangtze

Bangs, Richard, and Christian Kallen. *Riding the Dragon's Back: The Race to Raft the Upper Yangtze*. New York: Atheneum, 1988.

Barter, James. *The Yangtze*. Rivers of the World Series. Farmington Hills, Michigan: Lucent Books, 2003.

Bonavia, Judy. *The Yangzi River*. Revised by William Hurst. Lincolnwood (Chicago), Illinois: Passport Books, 1997.

Chan, Charis. *An Illustrated Guide to China*. Hong Kong: The Guidebook Company, 1988.

Chetham, Deirdre. *Before the Deluge: The Vanishing World of the Yangtze's Three Gorges*. New York: Palgrave MacMillan, 2002.

Danforth, Kenneth C. (editor). *Journey into China*. Washington, D.C.: National Geographic Society, 1976.

Eberhard, Wolfgang (editor). *Folktales of China*. New York: Pocket Books, 1973.

Hayman, Richard Perry. *Three Gorges of the Yangzi: Grand Canyons of China*. New York: Odyssey Publications, 2000.

Hersey, John. *A Single Pebble*. New York: Vintage Books, 1984.

Larmer, Brook. "Shanghai Dreams." *National Geographic*. Vol. 217 – No. 3 (March 2010), pp. 124–141.

Lynn, Madeleine (editor). *Yangtze River: The Wildest, Wickedest River on Earth*. New York: Oxford University Press, 1997.

Theroux, Paul. *Sailing through China*. Boston: Houghton Mifflin Company, 1983.

Van Slyke, Lyman P. *Yangtze: Nature, History, and the River*. Reading, Massachusetts: Addison-Wesley Publishing Company, 1988.

Wilkinson, Philip. *Yangtze*. London: BBC Books, 2005.

Winchester, Simon. *The River at the Center of the World: A Journey Up the Yangtze and Back in Chinese Time*. New York: Henry Holt and Company, 1997.

Wong, How Man. *Exploring the Yangtze: China's Longest River*. San Francisco, California: China Books & Periodicals, 1989.

Books

Aloian, Molly. *The Yangtze: China's Majestic River.* Rivers Around the World Series. New York: Crabtree Publishing Company, 2010.

Green, Jen. *National Geographic Countries of the World: China.* Washington, D.C.: National Geographic Children's Books, 2009.

Green, Jen. *Yangtze (Journey Along a River).* London: Hodder Wayland Childrens, 2009.

Kite, L. Patricia. *Building the Three Gorges Dam.* Chicago: Heinemann Raintree, 2011.

Leavitt, Amie. *Threat to the Yangtze River Dolphin.* Robbie Readers. Hockessin, Delaware: Mitchell Lane Publishers, 2008.

Meister, Cari. *Yangtze River.* Rivers and Lakes Series. Edina, Minnesota: Abdo Publishing Compamy, 2002.

Olson, Nathan. *The Yangtze River.* Land and Water series. North Mankato, Minnesota: Coughlan Publishing, 2004.

Simon, Charnan. *The Noble Yangtze.* Geography of the World Series. North Mankato, Minnesota: Child's World, 2004.

On the Internet

China Culture: Yangtze River
http://www.chinaculture.org/gb/en_travel/2003-09/24/content_34069.htm

Great Wall Across the Yangtze
http://www.pbs.org/itvs/greatwall/

Owen, Jerry. "Yangtze River"
http://www.africanwater.org/yangtze.htm

Rivers of Life: River Profiles – The Yangtze
http://cgee.hamline.edu/rivers/Resources/river_profiles/Yangtze.html

Spark, Nick T., and Others. "USS *Panay* – Suddenly and Deliberately Attacked!"
http://usspanay.org/attacked.shtml

amah (AH-mah)—An oriental female servant, especially a Chinese nurse

beneficent (buh-NEF-uh-suhnt)—generous, doing good

bund (bund)—An embanked thoroughfare along a river or the sea in the Far East

dynasty (DIE-nuh-stee)—A succession of rulers of the same line of descent

escarpment (e-SKAHRP-ment)—A steep slope at the edge of a plateau

facile (FA-suhl)—superficial, simple

inauspicious (in-aw-SPISH-us)—Not auspicious or showing signs of potential success

indigenous (in-DIJ-uh-nus)—Originating in and being produced, growing, living, or occurring naturally in a particular region or environment

irascible (i-RAA-suh-buhl)—hot-tempered, easily angered

junks (jungks)—flat-bottomed ships with sails, used in the China seas

kilowatts (KEE-luh-wot)—A thousand watts

Marxist (MAHRKS-ist)—One who follows the political and economic theory of Karl Marx, a German socialist writer (1818-1883), on which Communism is based

reach (reech)—A continuous extent, especially of water

sampans (SAM-panz)—Small flat-bottomed boats used along coasts and rivers of China

silt (SILT)—Sediment deposited by water in a channel or harbor.

terawatt (TER-uh-wot)—A trillion watts

tributary (TRIB-u-ter-ee)—A river or stream that flows into a large one or a lake

warlords (WOR-lord)—Military commanders exercising power by force over a certain region

yaks (yaks)—Long-haired oxen of central Asia

Index

ABOUT THE AUTHOR

Earle Rice Jr. is a former senior design engineer and technical writer in the aerospace, electronic-defense, and nuclear industries. He has devoted full time to his writing since 1993 and is the author of more than sixty published books. Earle is listed in *Who's Who in America* and is a member of the Society of Children's Book Writers and Illustrators, the League of World War I Aviation Historians, the Air Force Association, and the Disabled American Veterans.